POEMS ABOUT EDUCATION

POEMS FROM 'THE TEACHER' & 'EDUCATE' MAGAZINES

MICHAEL ROSEN

ILLUSTRATED BY TIM SANDERS

www.michaelrosen.co.uk/books

CONTENTS

INTRODUCTION

Over the last ten years I've been writing poems first for what was the National Union of Teachers magazine *The Teacher* and then for *Educate* the magazine of the new amalgamated teaching union, the National Education Union.

Some of the poems have been topical, some less so.

Feel free to use them in anyway you want. There's no charge or fee, but please remember that they are my copyright, so do please credit me.

THE TEACHER

Welcome to the new season of education ping-pong
played by politicians who are never wrong.

They come to the table with speeches and plans
whipping up support from their avid fans,
hoping that voters are simple-minded creatures
who think it's good to have a go at teachers.
In the blue corner we have Cameron and the Tories
who can't stop themselves telling the usual stories
about standards and failure – it's always the same
forever saying that it's teachers to blame . . .
even though teachers do what politicians command
they teach the curricula the politicians demand
working in the schools that the politicians create
whether it's a system teachers love or hate.

In time for the election, Cameron (such a creative bloke),
is going to play ping-pong with a brand new stroke:
It's 'Advisory Teachers', a Conservative invention
– though I have to say, I feel bound to mention
it was a system much used throughout the ILEA
a local authority which, as was their way,
the Tories abolished, because it got nothing right,
apart from this system, nicked for the election fight.

Yes, 'tis the season of education ping-pong
played by politicians who are never wrong.

But if you're thinking this is just a political stunt

then surely we'll do better with Tristram Hunt,
a man of learning who's studied the radical tradition –
after who came before, he's a welcome addition . . .
He'll know his job description is far too autocratic
he'll know running education must be democratic
From everything we've read in the papers about him
he'll say education can't be his personal whim.
So we waited with excitement for Hunt to serve
in the face of the Mail, he would hold his nerve
he would say education was too important a matter
to be left to politicians and Westminster chatter
he would say that teachers need to have a role
in shaping schools and education as a whole
he would know that it's not his job to preach
he'd know that his job is to help teachers teach.
Surely it would be one of his firm intentions
to talk of salary and teachers' pensions?
And come on, surely our Tristram Hunt would say
he was ending Performance Related Pay?

He raised his bat, would he spin, smash or both?
To everyone's amazement he uttered an oath.
Not an imprecation, obscenity or curse.
If anything, it was something worse.
Tristram told us he'd been on a tour
'I've been,' he said, 'to Singapore,
what they do is something we should imitate
if we want to put Britain back into the Great . . .
In Singapore', he said, 'teachers solemnly swear
to do their best, they promise they'll prepare
nice notes for their lessons, and I say today
that because Singapore is so like the UK
My policy'll be: 'What Singapore teachers do
The teachers I rule over will do too.'
Then, far and wide across the nation
all who work in education
found that they were of one mind
and uttered oaths of another kind.

Yes, 'tis the season of education ping-pong
played by politicians who are never wrong.

THE PAIN

Many of us in the world who never pray,
fell to our knees and were heard to say
'Whether there is a god – or not
now we know that we are shot
of Gove and his awful announcements
policy statements and lofty pronouncements,
may we be spared the constant preaching
on how to run schools, how to do teaching . . .'

But power does odd things to Oxbridge folk,
it seems to pump them up more than coke.
On a subject they have no expertise
they will appear totally at ease.
As expected, our optimism was shattered
when, Ms Morgan, you utterly battered
the concord between science and the arts
by saying science gives you the better start.

Didn't someone tell you it's not a competition
between Shakespeare's works and nuclear fission?
In a world beset with poverty and debt
we need all the wisdom we can possibly get.
We need scientists to discover and invent;
philosophers to explore our thought and intent;
artists to move us about the human condition,
and question the powerful who only know ambition.

The parts of education are not better or worse,
we can't improve the world with the old curse

of two cultures you've encouraged to compete.
That just takes us down a dead-end street.
If there isn't any Gove-ness you're going to revise
please spare us the pain of you trying to be wise

EDUCATION COMMANDMENTS

And when Moses came down from the Mountain,
the Prophet Michael asked of him, how many
Commandments do you have, and Moses replied verily,
'Have I ten' and then did Michael cry out, 'Ten! Is it not
eleven?' whereupon Michael pronounced an eleventh,
'Thou shalt convert'. Then did the people ask,
'Wherefore convert?' and Michael replied unto them
saying, 'For this way, in my Academies of Learning,
will all children become better'.

But then did the leader pronounce Michael as poison
and he was cast out into the wilderness to do with
his time nothing other than raising old members
from their slumbers.

Beyond the eyes of the people, however, Michael did
cause his eleventh commandment to be carried on by
those in his place, even as news came that not all those
who had converted to his Academies of Learning were
outstanding. Some forsooth needed improvement.
Yet others were failing.

Yea, verily, further news came from the land where such
Academies of Learning were legion, and the news was
not good for Michael: in this land, such Academies
were being struck down, for lo, the children had
not become better.

Whereupon Michael and his followers sayeth unto each other, 'Shhhhh, let not this matter be known.'

In Michael's place the Prophet Nicola came forth unto the people and spake wise words: 'No child can be left to linger in a House of Failure, nay, not for one day.'
But then did doubters come forth and ask Nicola how many of Michael's Academies of Learning were themselves Houses of Failure?

Then did she refuse to answer. Yea, verily, was she asked a second time, and then, again she answered not. Yea, verily, was she asked a third time, and then, again, she answered not. And thus it was seen on BBC Breakfast.

Then did the Prophet Nicola speak words exceeding strange. Again did she cry, 'No child can be left to linger in a House of Failure.'

And were the people not mystified by this, full of wonder that such ordure could be spoken by a Prophet.

Scholars come forth and revealed that out of the great Prophet Michael's Academies of Learning, were there 133 that were Houses of Failure.

And did not the people cry out in mocking ways, 'No child can be left to linger. Convert! Convert!'

But it was found that though the Eleventh Commandment stated 'Thou shalt convert', there was no Twelfth Commandment to state what these 133 Houses of Failure could convert to, for were they not already converted?

But the Prophet Nicola did not shake or tremble. And was it not then that the word 'brass neck' came into being?

Or 'chutzpah'.

Or both.

A NEW RULE

The sharpest minds from across the nation
have directed their attention to the situation
of giving education a new direction
in the troubled sphere of school inspection,
I hasten to point out, that this was not
a study commissioned to abolish the lot.
Why waste experience by creating an adviser
when everyone knows it's so much wiser
to harvest that knowledge to create instead
an esteemed inspector for Team Ofsted?

I'm afraid to say that results are persistent
in showing that Ofsted is inconsistent
In how it achieves its task of branding
England's schools as dud or outstanding.
Some might say that such crude grades
given on the basis of commando raids
is no way to make an evaluation
of something as complex as education.
Forget that! Never mind the pain
Inspection no good? Then do it again!

Astute thinkers, great minds hand-picked
have reached the conclusion they should inflict
a rule, that was learned from throwing dice
"If it fails once, then do it twice!"

A-LEVELS: TEACHING DISCRIMINATION

'Realising potential' – a motto to cherish:
teach by its aspiration – or perish.
'Realising potential' – a motto for today,
the inspiring axiom of AQA,
one of our great examination boards
stuffed with education's overlords
who rule and regulate what must be taught,
the courses and papers which must be bought.
Along with their colleagues, at OCR
they know it's time to raise the bar
to show the nation what's worth knowing,
what's to keep and what's for throwing.

The method they've used is called 'priorities',
what they've done is target minorities.
Learned people who know their stuff
say some languages aren't good enough.
So students fluent in Gujarati
Polish, Turkish or Punjabi
Bengali, Farsee or modern Hebrew,
many young bilingual students who
could get themselves a stunning grade
find instead they've been betrayed.

Blocked off from using what they know
many of these will not be slow
in figuring what the deal is here
the price they have to pay is dear:
languages in education come marked with a label

giving them positions in a language league table;
some hold a place as wisdom's fount
while others now just do not count.
This insight they now find is matched
by the fact that language comes attached
to people: families, students who
find themselves at the back of the queue.

This nugget of wisdom, you recognise
it leads your pupils to the highest prize:
doing the best they can possibly do
informed and supported in their work by you
All that it needs is that spark that fire
to lead them on, higher and higher.

WHAT SHORTAGE?

Field-Marshal Morgan sat in her tent,
looking at a map of the battle.
Behind her in his cot
General Gove was rattling his rattle.

A horse drew up outside.
A messenger dismounted.
He burst through the door and gasped,
'The numbers . . . they've been counted!'

The Field-Marshal didn't stir
her eyes barely flickered:
'This is the work of scare-mongers,'
good General Gibb snickered.

'There IS no shortage of troops,
I can assure you, Marm.
If there were, (which there isn't)
it's doom-sayers doing the harm.

We have hundreds of new recruits
and veterans returning to fight,
sergeants are in the colonies
recruiting day and night.'

Field-Marshal Morgan stood up
to address a newspaper man,
'Tell your readers at home
Everything's going to plan.'

'But, Marm,' said the newspaper man,
'may I be so bold as to mention
I'm hearing from the frontline
of a problem with retention.

You know the old saying?
Excuse me for saying it today
"Old soldiers never die
they simply fade away . . ." '

'Ignore him, Marm,' screamed Gibb,
'if troops are leaving the battle
it's 'cos they're not fit to fight.
And Gove rattled his rattle.

'Let's hold it there,' said Morgan
'time out, let's take a pause.
If there were by chance a shortage,
can anyone think of a cause?'

An injured veteran stood there
cleaning up around the camp,
he cleared his throat and moved
into the light of the lamp,

'For 20 years, Marm,
I've only heard one song:
"The troops we have are lousy,
everything they do is wrong.

The troops overseas are better
everywhere else is finer
No one can read and write,
And it's wonderful in China."

The only thing we can do
to make fighting men of these fools
is let anyone come along

and start up army schools.

We don't have to do very much
we can leave the rest to the press
to repeat and repeat and repeat
that the new schools are the best.

If this doesn't do the job
of increasing disaffection
we have something else:
a draconian system of inspection.

And while they're in the field
no soldier should ever be resting.'

FINE-LOOKING PLACES

Ladies and gentlemen, conjuring is an art,
when what we say, plays an important part.
Watch closely, see my fingers never leave my hand
Lights! Music! Let's hear it from the band!

I can see the expectation on your faces . . .
before your eyes, I reveal Fine-looking Places
created and owned entirely by you,
some old and revered, some brand new:
they're libraries, treasure houses of knowledge
stepping stones for life, leisure or college

And now, look closely, watch me reveal
something new, a thing of great appeal:
library tickets for all children in Year 3
watch them come out of the hat – do you see?
I'm sure I'm not doing any special pleading
when I say: "This is how we're encouraging reading."

But conjuring isn't just pulling things out of a hat
Come on! What would be the point of that?
It's also about what we can make disappear
Oh, come, come, there's nothing to fear,
but while you watched me pull the tickets out –
ah! you spotted it, a couple of you shout –
many of those Fine-looking Places that you rely on
aren't there anymore – phut! – they're gone.

Ladies and gentlemen that's the end of the show;

please show your appreciation as you go.
And remember, conjuring is an art
when what we say, plays an important part.

STUNNING LITERARY FIND: NEW LEWIS CARROLL 'ALICE' BOOK

Under the floorboards of a college room at Christ Church, Oxford, an electrician has found a manuscript thought to have been written by 'Lewis Carroll' (Charles Lutwidge Dodgson). Some of it is hard to decipher and it's clearly incomplete. Here's one passage:

'Come in,' said a woman in a loud voice.
Alice walked in to a large room at the Compartment of Edification.
Sitting in front of her, staring into the middle distance was the Blue Queen.
'How old are you?' said the Blue Queen.
'I'm seven years old,' said Alice politely.
Sitting next to the Queen was the Gibblet.
'Seven?' said the Gibblet, 'Seven? Test her.'
'Test her,' said the Blue Queen.
'Test me?' said Alice, 'but we've only just met.'
'And be robust,' said the Gibblet.
'And be robust,' said the Blue Queen.

Alice heard a scratching sound.
She looked round and observed a row of scribes scratching the word 'robust' on their scrolls.
'Why are you doing that?' enquired Alice.
'To tell the world the good news about robust tests,' they chorused.
'But how do you know 'Robust Tests' is good news?' asked Alice.
'Because the Blue Queen said it is,' chorused the scribes.
'Just because someone says something is something, doesn't mean that it is the thing they say it is,' said Alice.

'Test her!' shouted the Gibblet.

Test her!' shouted the Blue Queen.

'Robustly,' said the Gibblet.

'Robustly,' said the Blue Queen.

'Why do you keep repeating what he says?' said Alice.

'How else would I know what to say?' said the Blue Queen.

'You could think for yourself,' said Alice.

'No, no, no!' screamed the Gibblet. 'That's why we have the tests.'

'What? To help people think for themselves?'

'No, the opposite, you little ninny,' screamed the Gibblet.

'I like opposites,' said Alice. 'I like thinking of things that don't have opposites, like . . . a cupboard.'

'You go on like that, you'll fail the test,' laughed the Gibblet.

'You go on like that, you'll fail the test,' laughed the Blue Queen.

'As far as I'm concerned you've both failed,' said Alice.

She turned round and walked out.

A NEW MUCH IMPROVED 'HAMLET'

Hamlet stared at the SATs paper,
the question was extremely tough:
would he be right or wrong?
had he really studied enough?

The question said he must pick
one of two courses of action.
One way'd lead to disaster,
the other to satisfaction.

'I know I've got to choose
between "To be?" or "Not to be?"
That is the question,' he said,
'but it's much too hard for me.'

He argued with himself for a while,
he knew the choice was stark.
Then with a decisive move,
Hamlet finally made his mark.

It seems as if Hamlet's marker
was someone who yearned for fame.
He copied Hamlet's answer,
to use in his own name.

He wrote a play about a man
who kills his own brother
and Hamlet can't make up his mind
about one thing or another.

He wrote a speech for Hamlet
but stuck to the essential core:
no point in chat and debate
no one needs that anymore.

' "To be or not to be",
that's the question,' went the speech.
' "To be"'s the correct answer.
Now I'm off to the beach.'

The SATs showed this writer
that nothing should ever take long.
and everything in this world
is either right or wrong.

WE DO OUR BEST TO UNDERSTAND

We do our best to understand what politicians say;
we try to follow their thinking from day to day.
For some years now
they've explained why and how
English lessons had to be cut
teachers fired, colleges shut;
migrants learning English have been shown the door,
politicians explain there isn't the money anymore,
though some of us have stopped in our tracks
when we hear them say they can't collect tax
I mean to say, aren't you seriously bamboozled
our leaders can't get more tax out of Google?

And I know this doesn't come under the heading 'migration'
but when some of our banks went into administration
hadn't they 'migrated' billions out of here?
But hey, that was another time, another year,
and while we're on the subject of the 'other'
our leaders have discovered the 'Muslim Mother'
who, they say, 'is forced into segregation
by husbands opposed to integration,
what they need's a dose of education:
learn English or face deportation
talking foreign is causing a crisis:
they're packing their bags and joining Isis.'

Why let facts get in the way of a good story?
Talking like this may win election glory,
you're telling people to learn English somewhere

but it's your fault that the classes aren't there.
And apart from the job of whipping up hysteria
the truth about women who've gone to Syria
who have sadly chosen to go into this hell
is they seem to speak English extremely well.

On a related matter – it's a bit of a mystery
I'll have to include some personal history:
I can speak English, as you might have guessed
I've even passed the odd exam and test
but amazing to say, I have several great-grandmothers
who, along with most of their sisters and brothers
came to England hardly speaking a word
of English, I know this is absurd
but here's me reading and writing the stuff
I get by . . . as you can see, I'm good enough

How come my family learned English in a generation?
How did this happen without threat of deportation?
Though you won't be surprised to know
at the time some people had 'evidence' to show
that deep in east London, there was something alarming
many Jewish mothers were seriously harming
the nation's gene pool, by not knowing how
to speak English! Seems like then as now.

We do our best to understand what politicians say;
we try to follow their thinking from day to day.

ENGLISH SYSTEMS

It was late at night – the candle was burning low,
fault lines in the cabinet were beginning to show,
outside on the street hacks were getting curious,
alone in her office, Nicky Morgan was furious.
Bit by bit she'd come to the realisation
that Osborne would announce academisation:

'This isn't justice, it's nothing less than a perversion
It was MY job to announce the forced conversion
How dare he put that in his budget speech?
It's my job to teach teachers how to teach
I thought that Osborne was my best mate
What am I? Secretary of Getting in a State?'

That was back in March, events are moving faster
Nicky Morgan's job is turning into a disaster:

'PM promised it was my moment of glory,
yet some who are against it have always voted Tory
PM said I could prove I showed 'relevance'
but the press keep saying, 'Show us the evidence!'
Does it really matter that I haven't got any?
This is how we rule: the few over the many.
Surely it can't be so very wrong o'me
to compel all schools to have autonomy?
Some people say we sound like aristocrats:
but just you see, we'll abolish the bureaucrats.
All bureaucracy, we're magicking away
putting in its place on 'special' pay

experts, tooled up like Roman legions,
'School Commissioners' to roam the regions
while all academies and academy chains
'reward' their managements for holding the reins.'

But Nicky's not alone in selling this stuff,
they know that even she is not enough.
It isn't easy selling such a big fib
So into the breach steps Minister Gibb:
'Two systems are bad. We must have ONE system!'

But England loves systems, Nick must have missed'em,
like: the ones where you pay to go to school
learn the technique of how to rule.
'Independent', 'Public' or 'denominational'
'Academy Free Schools' or 'vocational'
tucked in corners, tutors or crammers
or in several counties, the good old grammars.
Does all this mean we're heading in the direction
of bringing back grammars, bringing back selection?

I'll keep it simple, we understand the plans:
they want to take schools out of our hands.
Our ownership of schools will henceforth cease:
a hundred and twenty five year lease
replaces a silly old-fashioned situation,
where we the people owned education.

THE SOCIAL LADDER

"Today we offer you social mobility.
Do you possess extreme agility?
Are you willing to devote some time?
Do you think you have the ability to climb?

We'd like you to think that above you there sit
places for lower-class people who'll fit
because, don't you know, the recentest trend
is for upper-class people to choose to descend?

They respect the fact that you're living in hope.
For you they'll slide down the slippery slope,
They'll do that sort of thing because they're nice
they believe in the value of self-sacrifice."

Though we don't have a real aristocracy
nor do we have what they call meritocracy.
With inherited wealth, private education
and tax avoidance, it's a divided nation.

The reason they offer us social mobility
is to stop us thinking about social equality;
they want us to think everyone will go far
so that we'll accept things just as they are.

HURRAH FOR THE CONQUERORS

Archaeologists working in a London suburb have found a manuscript that appears to be the words of a school song sung by pupils at the William the Conqueror Grammar School in the 1950s.

Hurrah for the Conquerors
the finest in the land;
we're here to be the best
make our mark in the sand.
We're glad they created
the noble grammar school
that way they put in place
the law of divide and rule.

We strive to be the best,
only the best is good for us,
Who cares about the rest,
for we passed the 11-plus?
When it rains upon the world,
it's others who get sodden.
God bless Conqueror Grammar,
but not the Secondary Modern.

We work hard in our studies,
we fight on the playing field;
proud at the age of 11
our fate was forever sealed.
Where would the country be,

as the world's greatest nation,
if there wasn't school selection,
and constant segregation?

A GAME OF TABLES

Does society shape the education it needs?
Does the education system shape society?
The people who compile international tables
aren't very interested in this kind of complexity.

They want us to accept league table positions
as if these are judgements on pure education
with no reference or application that comes
from considerations of a culture or nation.

The tables tell us, the compilers inform us,
how to run classrooms, how to run schools
with no link to the societies that produce them.
Is this because they think we are fools?

Wouldn't it be useful to pause and think
and consider for a moment what kinds of society
produce the winners on education tables
and might not that give us a degree of anxiety?

Might it not be that league table success
can be bought with authoritarianism?
Might it not be that this kind of 'ism'
matches up nicely with totalitarianism?

But hey, let's ignore that kind of stuff!
Education must be measured by competition:
nation versus nation all over the world,
based on education league table position.

We can easily dispose of debate and discussion;
dispense with argument, the arts and dissent;
all we need are league table performers:
education should only aim for more per cent.

THE CHAIR

In London W11
a school.
In the school
a room.
In the room
a chair.
A chair that is empty.
A chair that waits.

But no one comes.
The chair is empty.

Here come words.
Words are flying.
The air is full of words,
and the words float down,
down on to the chair.
The chair
in the room.
The room
in the school.
The school
in London W11.

SPENDING LESS

O teachers, teachers how little you understand
of the thought put into what's been planned.
If schools find there's less money to go round
why assume you're being run into the ground?

Think of yourselves as if you're on a mission:
if you have less money, you'll be more efficient.
Instead of complaining, moaning and bleating
why don't you turn down the central heating?

Where's the evidence you have to be hot
to teach a book or follow a plot?
Never forget we're up against economic rivals:
education should be a matter of survival.

Do you really need to take them on trips?
Economize, stupid! Read my lips.
That counsellor, that flashy drama production:
remember, we get fitter through weight reduction.

Look in your pigeon holes I'm sending out a letter:
"Spending less on schools makes education better."

THE TWENTY-FIVE PER CENT

Remember how Cameron stood before us and roared:
– A quarter of all children are not reading properly!
And the media trumpeted these statistics too;
and the whole country wept at such a sad story . . .

But help was at hand, the Tories knew best:
phonics first, fast and only would solve the problem
and a government expert was hired to advise.
She advised that the government pay 50%
of the cost of the phonics schemes which she wrote
and all would be well in the world of reading.

To prove that progress was happening – and fast –
the government devised a Phonics Screening Check
which would show that the children could 'decode'
it would show they'd learned the 'alphabetic code'

And they did: the phonics teaching taught the phonics
the children learned how to say the words out loud
and everyone said, it's working, yes it's working.

But we know that the government dearly loves testing
and at Key Stage 2, they like to test 'Reading'.
This is that thing where we don't say words out loud,
we understand the words we see on the page.
And we waited in hope and expectation for the results
and heavens alive, how excited we were to see . . .

. . . a quarter of all children were not reading properly!

Only three quarters reading at the expected level!

And some of us are waiting for the media trumpets
to tell the country to weep at this story . . .
After all, it's our money that's been pumped in to schools
to buy the schemes that would improve the reading
Surely this'd be a national scandal and disaster
a conspiracy of teachers wickedly depriving
the disadvantaged of the right to be fluent readers.

But no . . . not a thing, all quiet on that front,
All's well, nothing to talk about here, so carry on.

SONNET: LOOKING BOTH WAYS

Ministers talk about the 'high skills economy',
desperately needed for Brexit autonomy.
Pressure on teachers and students mounts,
(they say every point on PISA counts)
and yet this demand for the highest performance
is undermined by the kind of ordinance
which keeps gurus of the free market mollified
by saying that teachers don't have to be qualified.

So who cares if students, fearful of debt,
think that university's too risky a bet?
But demands for high skills is most contradicted
by education cuts the government has inflicted.

This is not a drive towards a new meritocracy;
it's just a display of good old hypocrisy.

NICE WORK IF YOU CAN GET IT

If you're feeling that the end is near,
and you'd rather have another career,
don't be afraid of being seen as a defector
you could have a go at being an inspector.
If that doesn't appeal, how's this instead?
Why not aim higher: be Head of Ofsted?
This could be the job that's made for you
if you like blaming people
– for what they were told to do.

You've seen your colleagues doing their best
preparing pupils for every kind of test;
you'll know how hard you yourself strove
to jump through hoops put there by Gove.
For Head of Ofsted, the job specification
will be to blame teachers for the education
that Michael Gove told you all to 'deliver'.
Do it with emotion – cry me a river,
this shows the media you're really caring.
A few weeks later, try something daring.
Pick your moment, don't be hasty,
have a go at Health and Safety.
Call schools 'risk-averse', you can be quite rude,
even though they live in fear of being sued.

Deliver these thoughts as speeches to the nation
(you mustn't waste time with co-operation)
and that's the path you should try to tread
if the job you're going for is: Head of Ofsted.

THE BALLAD OF UNKNOWING

Up and down the country,
head teachers up in arms,
saying cuts in budgets
are causing untold harm.

Schools asking parents
to pay for books and glue;
TAs are being fired . . .
. . . but is it really true?

Mr Gibb has the answer,
don't say he's trying to fudge it.
He says: 'Read my lips
there are no cuts to the budget.'

Mr Gibb says that schools
don't know what they know.
We must believe what he says
because he's told us so.

We're in new territory here,
the future is the past.
A is B and you are me
through a looking-glass.

Altering our reality
is something of a mission,
but it's all in a day's work
when you're a politician.

THE 11-PLUS

The 11-plus is coming back (thanks to an extra £50 million being fed into grammar schools) and it'll always have aspects that are unfair, unequal and it's a false predictor anyway.

One great advantage of getting old:
you think you might just as well be bold.
If a minister gives us a rehashed 11-plus
I feel like telling how it was for us.

Before our final year at school
they applied the usual ability rule:
divided us into Class A and B
said there was no difference we could see.
But some of us had hands, they said
while others (in Class A), had heads.

I was in Class A, each week we had tests
to find out who was worst, who best.
Then our scores were averaged out
and just in case there was any doubt
we were given 'places' around the class
and Miss told us which of us would pass.
She stood in the middle, arms out wide
'All of you will pass, on this side . . .'
She turned around, like a windmill sail
and said, 'All on this side – will fail!'

The certainty of this, with no room for error
filled me with a feeling of terror.
At English I was dead cert OK
but maths I was certain fail, all day.
I had a sense I was like the Titanic
heading for the iceberg in a state of panic.
I learned how this realisation bites:
you end up with sleepless nights.

When it came to the exam, I think I failed
but I didn't know what it all entailed.
My Mum, aware of my consternation,
found out I was given 'headteacher's recommendation'.

But my friend, Brian, about the same level as me
failed the exam – but then I could see
no 'recommendation' for a builder's son.
In the race for the 'Grammar', he lost, I won,
which felt like the path to hell or heaven
and it was all decided by the age of 11.
And why was I one of the lucky creatures?
I forgot to say, both my parents were . . . teachers!

BOLD BEGINNINGS

It seems like the people at the head of education
have been overwhelmed by some alliteration
batting for Ofsted, in what's been a long innings
they've produced a report, called 'Bold Beginnings'.
It gives an account of an exciting conception:
a vision for four-year-olds, a curriculum for reception.
Please take a read, it's found at gove.uk
and see the doubt cast on children's 'free play',
as something useless, to be thought of with suspicion
not a part of socialisation, or even cognition.
No discussion here of what's in a child's mind
instead they're worried about who 'falls behind'
and yet the tests and exams which now prevail
determine there's a percentage who have to fail.
Rather than worry about fixing children with labels
children know they're sitting at fast and slow tables
and if anyone in education is keen on betting
the odds are now that reception will use setting:
four-year-olds sorted, sieved and selected
marked and graded, and – with luck – inspected;
and in a flourish that seems designed to please,
the report reminds us: it's all about the GCSEs!

Four-year-olds, listen!
Stop your foolish play.
Those GCSEs
aren't far away.

MIDAS

We know that some of you are rightly concerned
our education boats might have been burned,
'cos the pace of teacher recruitment lags
behind the rate of teachers packing their bags.

But I'm not going to give time or room
to all you pessimistic prophets of doom,
nor will I shmooze you with any soft soap,
for today I bring you a message of hope.

Of course, we could find there may be gaps;
the flow of schooling may occasionally lapse,
but rest assured there'll be no diminution
we've been working on a serious solution
to any problems arising from poor supply
or a slowdown in people wanting to apply.
Ladies and gentlemen, the world is turning
to the power and beauty of digital learning.

I'm not just thinking of it as a handy assistant,
geeing up the student who's a little bit resistant,
a bit of technology to win over the creatures.
No, my friends! I mean replacing teachers.
Please, no disrespect, no need to laugh
but I have a dream: schools with no staff!

The morning bell rings, the students jog in,
the tablets are running, the students log in,
each step in learning is meticulously guided.

And thanks to the digital services provided,
any behavioural problems, we will see
thanks to the presence of the CCTV,
digitally locking on to any student's face
observed by the officer in the surveillance base.

Thanks for listening and I really think
we should also give thanks to Midas Inc.
and to all those ministers of extraordinary ability
who've put Midas on the road to profitability.

THE COST OF COMPETITION

Modern education has a great new tradition:
putting schools through inter-school competition.
I'm not talking here about inter-school sports,
the people in charge have much greater thoughts:
the quality of education will improve, they say,
if children compete in a more radical way,
one that requires grand-looking databases
as the children are forced to compete for places
like shows where prizes are awarded to cattle.
Schools have to fight in a Places Battle
though in some localities it's more like a war.
"We're much better than the school next door
and just to prove it, we hire people to devise
shiny banners and posters which advertise
the absolute fact it's 100% true
we do things much better than other schools do."

Now there's nothing wrong with a bit of pride
though perhaps it's better worn on the inside
but all this boasting and self-justification
has to be added to the cost of education,
and if we bring to this discussion a bit of reality
just think about all schools in your locality:
(far be it from me to hit a note of dissent)
but couldn't that money be much better spent?

BASELINE BOTHERATION

Sad to say, this is a report on the addiction
of those who think they have the power of prediction,
based on what is nothing more than a perception
that tests administered to kids in reception
will enable DfE to compare schools' proficiency
in helping children to progress, with efficiency.

A panel of experts said the tests are unreliable,
yet governments are always, we know, very liable
to use such data to hold schools to account,
particularly whenever they want to mount
a case to alter a school's composition.
Such drastic measures would be a poor decision:
assessment for young children is best when it's formative,
they don't need this addiction to tests that are normative.

Anyone serious about our children's education
knows very well that a genuine evaluation
would not be possible till the end of Key Stage 2 –
that's not till 2027, between me and you.

Ten million quid is what the tests are going to cost:
that's more money for schools, that we know will be lost.

A SPOKESPERSON ON DISABILITY SPEAKS THEIR MIND

"You may have thought that schools had less to spend
on staff, music, school trips and facilities;
less to spend on children with 'Special Educational
Needs and Disabilities'.
You may have imagined that there is an increase in
demand and an upward tick in prices;
you may have got the wrong end of the stick and
imagined there's some kind of crisis.

Indeed if you look in the papers there's a comment
from the Minister for Children you may have found:
"We have taken a number of steps to help schools
get the best value for every pound."
I think you'll agree this proves the point that all is
well for schools in this matter
and the suggestion that there's a problem
is nothing but scaremongering and idle chatter.

Let's remember that this is a new kind of world
we must face up to the challenges we're going to meet.
We can't be feather-bedded, or mollycoddled,
we have to be ready to stand on our own two feet.
This may well mean that many of the children who
come into the category of SEND
may discover later that their disability is not so bad
and that they are on the mend.

Surely no one says the disabled should think that
they are exempt from any kind of test,

after all this Government is proud to have made
it necessary for the disabled to be reassessed.
This way we've found that many adults who were
'disabled' were in fact lazy and inclined to shirk.
And our reassessment procedures have enabled
such people to get into work.

To our credit, this has significantly
cut the benefits bill, we have said
even if this has in part resulted from
the fact that some of the people
were dead.
So you can see from this that
our approach to the disabled
in education
is a policy that operates consistently
for all ages across the nation."

STRESS

Damian Hinds, Secretary of State for Education, said: 'When you leave school, hard and stressful things come along. Learning about what can be stressful episodes is part of the preparation for later life.'

Out there in the real world we can get in a mess,
sometimes things hit us, we get really stressed.
But listen up teachers, you know the situation,
whatever's bad in life, you should put in education.

Out there in life, you may have nothing to eat,
make it easy on the kids, something to repeat.
Listen to me now, stop playing the fool,
don't give hungry kids food in school.
Let them learn now when they're really young,
how you're so hungry, you could eat your tongue.

And look, everyone knows that work can be boring,
you'd rather be at home, in bed asleep snoring.
Don't leave it to chance or every now and then,
make school boring forever again and again.

TEACHER RETENTION: PROBLEM SOLVED

Teacher retention's a tricky situation.
If we're going to solve it, we need imagination.
There's really no point in taking the easy road:
like coming up with ways to cut workload.
There's really no point in doing boring stuff:
like paying teachers more or paying them enough.
All this does is appeal to teachers' greed,
we need something we're sure is bound to succeed.
Something to do with time and space,
something to keep teachers in their place.

Let's think this through with a bit of maturity:
we've learnt a lot about domestic security.
Cameras surround some people's homes,
they have electronic gates and entryphones.
Perhaps hired secret guards hide in a bin
so whoever's outside, can't get in.
Which could also mean – have no doubt –
whoever's inside, can't get out.
Now – yes – owners with their codes and keys
can come and go, just as they please . . .

. . . but start thinking now in an original way:
it's half past three, the end of the day;
you watch your students as they all leave . . .
. . . the DfE sends a message for all to receive,
then – in an instant – just as you might suppose
across the land school gates start to close.
There's no time to get out, no chance to hide

and all the teachers end up locked inside
so, as easy as you like, no fuss no fight,
the teachers stay in all through the night.

And that is how, with the minimum of tension,
we solve the crisis of teacher retention.

NO CUTS

There was a whisper and a rumour going round the DfE:
"There are teachers, there are parents who have started to see
that when people in the country who are mostly fairly wise
say schools are facing cuts, then it really isn't lies."

So lunchtime was cancelled, the staff stopped their eating
Everyone was summoned to a departmental meeting.
A mandarin stood up and explained why they were there
"It may not be nice, my friends, and it may not be so fair
but the truth is in the open and it's running very fast
the population out there are getting it at last.
So who's got a plan that we can quickly put in place?
Don't ask if it works, ask: will it save our face?"

There was silence in the room, as no one really knew
what measures could be taken, what anyone could do
until, that is, a fresh-faced man, with an Oxford degree
(best not to say he'd never taught, on that we can agree),
raised his hand in the air and was called upon to speak,
he was nervous and a rosy flush spread across his cheek:
"I don't want to put anyone's nose out of joint
but I think that people here are missing the point.
You see, it isn't really necessary to have butter on your toast
when I look at education, I ask: what is it costs the most?
I've got the figures here, I've got every statistic
Don't you think it's time the DfE got realistic?
We have the expertise, we have the technology
we need a shift in our mindset, a shift in psychology
our funds are very limited, not endlessly elastic

We have to move now, do something very drastic
Of course we love the workforce, they are hardworking creatures,
but the time has come at last to get rid of all the teachers."

Our Oxford man sat down, his face flushed and pink;
what he said reverberated; people paused a mo to think.
He may be young, they thought, and wet behind the ears
but surely this was wisdom that was far beyond his years.

An instruction went out; and up the department ladder;
the suits at the top couldn't possibly be gladder.
With a pace that was measured, in a tone that was polished
the minister announced: "Teachers are abolished!"
The burden on Government spending was instantly reduced
and as I'm sure you've figured, as I'm sure you've just deduced
it was now possible to declare – with no ifs, and no buts
there were now, once and for all: absolutely no cuts.

OUR BEST HAS NOT BEEN GOOD ENOUGH

Teachers!
Go out and tell the children
the way the world is.
Go out and tell the children
that this is the way
we made the world.

But what if the children ask us
if the way the world is
is not good enough?
What if the children ask us
if the way you made the world
is not good enough?

Tell them that we are the people
who know best.
Tell them that we are the people
who have always known best.
Tell them that we have told you
to tell the children this.

But what if the children say
they have seen what's coming?
What if the children say
that when they are old
you will be gone?
What if the children say
that they don't want
to live and die in a desert?

What if the children say
that your best has not
been good enough?
What if the children say
it's nearly too late?

HOW DO WE KNOW?

How do we know what we know?
How do we find new things to know?

Alessandro Giuseppe Antonio Anastasio Volta
heard that something odd happens
if your tongue touches a piece of metal
just as that metal is touching a piece
of a different metal: a sour taste.

Alessandro Giuseppe Antonio Anastasio Volta
thought he'd try out some stuff.
He put a silver coin on top of his tongue
and a piece of tinfoil under it.
When he made the tinfoil touch the silver coin
the sour taste happened.
Why? he wondered.
He figured that it wasn't because
of something in him,
it was because of things
that could be found in metal and spit.
He had discovered that
when you have the right stuff
you can make electricity.

Alessandro Giuseppe Antonio Anastasio Volta
played with stuff
in order to find things out.

Molte grazie, Alessandro,
thank you very much.

THE BUS GOES ON

The bus goes on and it's full and it's leaving
and it's laughing and it's going on and it's morning
and it's evening and it's in Punjabi
and it's daytime and it's full and it stops
and it's suspicious and it starts and
it's in Ibo and it's shouting and it's shopping
and it's rapping and it's lit up and it's dark
and it's 'Shove up!' and it's crying and it's
squealing and it's in Dutch and it's braking
and it's in Geordie and it's at the station
and it's skint and it's full of babies and it's
full of men and it's going on and it's past
the Vietnamese café and it's past the tyre depot
and it's past the silver car and its chauffeur
and it's waiting for Sinatra to start up and
it's in patois and it's chips and vinegar and
it's past the park and it's full of football and
it's a bellyache and it's full of jokes and it's
scared and it's in Arabic and it's back from
school and it's pushing and it's raining and
it's ripe armpits and it's 'tranks' and it's angry
And it's full of yesterday and it's riding under
The lights and it's pissed off and it's smell of oil
and it's lean and it's combing and it's kissing
and it's packets of rice and it's cassava and
it's over the canal and it's the baby's bottle
and it's over the railway and it's under the cranes
and it's in the shadows of the palaces in glass
and it's in Albanian and it's bleach and it's the

homework in late and it's spuds and it's the hijab
and it's shoulders next to back next to fronts
and it's revving and it's too late and it's too early
and it's not enough and it's going on and it's on
time and it's dreaming and it'll get there today
and it'll get there tomorrow…

ISOLATION

When our society creates areas
where there is little hope,
we ask for schools and teachers
to get on and cope.
When society spends less
on providing education,
we ask schools and teachers
to make good the situation.

Then the word comes down
to every school and college
that the time has come
to deliver more knowledge.
This has to be restricted
to the kind you can measure,
which means much more testing
and much more pressure.

There are students who crack
in this dire situation
But a solution's been found:
put these folk in isolation.
So the ills of society
that have been brewing for years
we solve by putting youngsters
alone with their fears.

We're following the path
we follow again and again:
we get hold of the victims
and make them take the blame.

THESE ARE THE HANDS

These are the hands
That touch us first
Feel your head
Find the pulse
And make your bed.

These are the hands
That tap your back
Test the skin
Hold your arm
Wheel the bin
Change the bulb
Fix the drip
Pour the jug
Replace your hip.

These are the hands
That fill the bath
Mop the floor
Flick the switch
Soothe the sore
Burn the swabs
Give us a jab
Throw out sharps
Design the lab.

And these are the hands
That stop the leaks
Empty the pan

Wipe the pipes
Carry the can
Clamp the veins
Make the cast
Log the dose
And touch us last.

WHAT YOU DON'T KNOW

As the Covid pandemic rages across the nation,
perhaps now's a good time to try imagination:
we know that politicians have begun conversations
on whether it would be right to delay examinations.

But let's imagine this could be a moment of unity:
instead of being a problem, it could be an opportunity.
A window has opened, it's a time we could seize:
and ask the question, why do we have GCSEs?

Five years of education reduced to a few hours race
to scribble as much as possible at a frightening pace.
In fact, quite often it doesn't matter how fast you go
what they seem to be testing is what you don't know.

Now of course this suggestion often causes anxiety
but what if we mixed examinations with more variety?
School time research, course work that's invigilated?
Marking by teachers that's rigorously moderated?

Getting this to be debated always takes nerve
it's often resisted by lovers of the bell curve,
the system that ranks according to a norm
but hey, isn't now a good time, to kick up a storm?

TO THE GOVERNMENT

Is it really too much to ask
that you lay down instructions
about wearing a mask?

Making such things a matter of choice
is simply a way
of not using your voice.

Wearing masks is a social act.
Leaving it to chance
has no basis in fact.

Social medicine has to involve us all
or the preventative project
is bound to fall.

You have flirted with eugenics
with your 'herd immunity'
like it's a bag of tricks.

Was it right, ethical or fair
to shunt old people
out of hospitals into care?

That caused thousands to die
and the lack of protective gear
made us all ask why?

And now you send us back to school

with half-hearted measures.
Do you take us for fools?

I write this as someone who got ill
I've suffered from what it's caused
and always will.

PLAN? WHAT PLAN?

This feels like a good time to try to remember
that time way back in early September
it was totally in the government's hands
to have given us right then a set of plans
to cover what was a predictable situation
of big gaps in attendance across the nation.

Last year's disaster may sit on their conscience,
so will we be spared the algorithm nonsense
of marking students based on the distribution
of grades from previous years, as a solution?

Students and teachers should have been told
what to expect, not left out in the cold.

Even now the idea of what would be best
are agreed ways for students to be assessed
so that we can sort out our expectations
without the usual one-off examinations.

Yet again these battles will have to be fought
even as the curriculum is being taught.
Will they issue an edict as an act of governance?
Will it be dictatorship through their incompetence?

MORE FOR LESS

'The exams are cancelled!' the Great Man said,
though no one knew what we'd have instead.
Commentators scanned the Great Man's features:
did he really mean they would trust the teachers?

Would they accept that teachers really can tell
which students struggle, which are doing well?
For one brief moment, this seemed the logical route
but with the hand of trust, then came the boot.

Schools had to prove their testing was reliable
and although their rigour was undeniable,
the pressure was on to provide more evidence:
exams were replaced by series of 'assessments'.

While teachers did the setting and marking of these,
schools went on paying the exam boards their fees.
Teachers who mark exams to top up their pay,
discovered it wouldn't be coming their way.

Figuring what's going on is anyone's guess
but the result is the usual: work more for less.

WAY BACK IN SEPTEMBER

Way back in September
when the weather was sunny and bright,
we thought it would be fairly easy
for the Government to get it right.

Surely they could easily predict
without being clever or wise
that schools would have to close
as Covid infections would rise?

So would they be able to deduce
that pupils would spend more hours
having to study at home?
Was that beyond the Government's powers?

Yet it seems to have been impossible
to solve a problem quite so mighty
or they would have made really sure
that ALL pupils had the right IT.

It's hard to avoid the conclusion
that they were indeed aware
but as they didn't do the job
they're a Government that doesn't care.

CATCHING UP

To make it possible for us to work as a society
It seems as if we need to have social anxiety
An idea or feeling becomes a widespread trope
The latest being said is that children can't cope
In itself this probably isn't anything very new
but now, 'they have a lot of 'catching up to do'.

'Longer school days!' a gaggle of experts cry
'Shorter holidays!' one shouts, 'give that a try!'
'Teachers! Work harder!' then reaches our ears.
Or, 'Now let's recruit an army of volunteers!'
Apart from the fact that this is all crazy
It fits the myth that teachers are all lazy.

There's also the myth that teachers are jugs
While children walk about being empty mugs
So these mugs (their brains) teachers have to fill
Because during lockdown children stood still.
They didn't talk or think or read or play,
They sat like lemons day after day.

Some experts seem to go further, I think:
They reckon children's brains have started to shrink.
Amidst all this talk of children 'falling behind'
shouldn't we think about what is the mind?
How much 'catching up' can a young brain take?
Maybe emergency cramming's a big mistake.

IN CASE OF
'LAZY' TEACHER
BREAK GLASS

SQUALOR

The Guardian, Aug 28, 2021:

England's schools in urgent need of repairs, say heads. Teachers tell
of leaking ceilings, broken heating, inadequate ventilation, as leaders
say they have no money to fix problems

Do you remember those great school trips,
away for a week, outward bound
learning and exploring, map in hand,
walking miles on muddy ground?

We headed off in hired coaches
singing our way to a distant place:
a special centre where we'd meet
the trained warden with the smiley face.

Forget it, folks! For now there's no need
for all that effort and expense
you can get as good much cheaper,
an experience just as intense.

If you want to face the elements
or get that outdoor feeling
then stay in school, you can get it there
the rain is coming through the ceiling.

Everyone can wear their waterproofs
and study the cracks on the walls.
When they skid on the soaking floors
they can study the effects of falls.

We're back to J.K. Galbraith's words
when he looked at who got the dollar:
while some build up their private wealth
we get public squalor.

WE ARE BRITAIN

The Department for Education has circulated a new anthem that they wanted schools to sing on June 25th. By the time it got to Michael Rosen, the words seemed to have changed...unless it was him who changed them...

We are Britain
And we have one dream
To disunite people
in the same team

Verse 1:
Our nation survived through many storms and wars
We've opened our doors, and widened our island's shores
But if you look closely, you'll see how we start
to divide and rule, keeping people apart

Chorus:
We are Britain
And we have one dream
To disunite people
Until they scream

Verse 2:
So many different people, standing in one nation
but not much fun, if you're the Windrush generation
While the House of Commons committee on education
pits people against people suffering deprivation.

Chorus:
We are the government
We could be comedians
so we think you won't notice
we cut pupil premiums

Outro:
Strong Britain, Great Nation
Stirring up Britain, Misinformation
Wrong Britain, Repatriation
So long, Britain, Disintegra-a-tion

LEVELLING DOWN

Facts and figures can often say a lot
about what is the truth and what is not.
I was listening to the radio the other day
I was sure that I heard a woman say
in the year ending in March, 400 or more
nurseries closed. And there was more in store:
one third of these was in areas the most deprived.
Hold it, I thought, hasn't a new era arrived?
Aren't we 'levelling up', abolishing the 'poverty trap'?
Isn't the boast, 'We're closing the attainment gap'?

Nurseries are the foundations of what comes later
again and again we've been told they must cater
for all, free for most or exceedingly cheap
not provided at rates which for most are too steep.
otherwise the poor are simply kept outside,
that attainment gap is kept permanently wide.
I remember a time when we talked of compensation
the disadvantaged would get more education.
The truth is clear, as anyone can guess
Those who have little are going to get less.

PARTY TIME

Children! Gather round and learn from your betters.
Listen to our leaders, the great men of letters.
They teach us many things concerning what's right.
They are beacons in the sky, we follow their light.

As you know, dear children, we show you what's best
Life is like a river, it's a constant test.
We are inspired from on high from people we admire
so we too can aim high, and then go higher.

We are lucky where we live, we are ruled over by the great:
People in love with truth, steering the ship of state.
We trust them to make rules, rules that will protect us
these are the bonds, the ties that connect us.

It goes without saying that these rules once made
are rules for them too, always to be obeyed.
And just as we teach you, to be honest and true
so then are our rulers an example to you.

A LETTER

For Holocaust Memorial Day (27 January) I recounted how I had
lost relatives to the Nazi persecution of Jews during World War II.
The following poem is written as a letter to my father's uncle, Oscar,
who was a watchmaker.

Dear Oscar, what did you think as you and Rachel sat on the floor of the cattle
truck as it left Paris?
Did you think of the watches and clocks you had mended?
Did you think of the tiny springs and wheels?
You, with your magnifying glass in your eye, pouring over the works so that a
monsieur or a madame could tell the time correct to the exact second.
Did you look through the gaps in the slats on the side of the truck?
Did you see farmers in fields, women selling clothes in a market?
Did you call out?
Did you push your hands through the gaps?
Did the night come creeping in?
Did you see a light from a window where people sat and ate their evening meal?
Did you see, in the dark, horror on Rachel's face?
Did she see horror on yours?
Did you shut her eyes?
Did she shut yours?
Thinking of children who shut their eyes to make the world go away.
And then, behind your eyelids, did you think of the cattle that had once stood
in the truck as they were taken away to the slaughterhouse?

THE NEW REALITY

How worrying it must be to be in power
when children watch the news hour by hour.
Take as one example the lockdown time,
when a breach of the rules, earned you a fine;
you and your family didn't have 'dos',
kept all meetings, down to twos;
missed out on seeing Gramps and Nan
you did what was best, as part of the plan.

Then you turn on your TV and you quickly hear
that those in power, only last year,
were gathering together – women and men
for drinks and laughs, at Number 10.

But hold it right there! There is much concern
that children, knowing this, might speak out of turn.
Horror of horrors! Children have written letters
that seem to criticise their powerful betters –
letters written by children, in their schools
about those who broke the lockdown rules.

Luckily, the response has been sharp and clear
from those in power who bend our ear.

Such letters will have no place in the new reality
we must, in future, show political impartiality.

PIE CHARTS OR PIES?

In a speech at Conservative Party conference, former Prime Minister Liz Truss said: 'For too long, the political debate has been dominated by how we distribute a limited economic pie. Instead, we need to grow the pie so that everyone has a bigger slice.'

For years we've been teaching a special art:
how to show distributions with a pie chart.

Those in charge must have been paying attention:
pie charts are back in, getting a mention.

Though the talk has shifted from pie charts to pies;
they say, 'Don't talk of portions, it's all about size.

'It's the size of the pie that matters most,' they say,
that's why they tell us to not talk about pay!

While we have to live with a huge rise in prices,
they're busy saying, 'Ignore pie chart slices.'

And we can see more coming up on the pie chart:
they also want to cut the welfare part!

So we have to take action and this is how:
we have a demand: pay up and pay up now.

HEATWAVE (JULY 18 & 19, 2022)

The sun was rising high in the sky,
sweat was dripping off the wall.
The children were slumped in their chairs,
the air was heavy in the hall.

'Oh no!' the head was gasping
as he sipped cold water from his cup
'I've looked at the weather forecast:
The temperature is going up!'

'I'll get on the phone to Ofsted
and ask them to postpone the inspection.
They'll agree to that I'm sure
after a few moments of reflection.'

Later that day, at the staff meeting
the head had to deliver a warning
'it's all going to get hotter:
Ofsted'll be here in the morning!'

THE BLACK HOLE MYSTERY

You can always tell, when things are getting serious,
politicians make the economy seem strangely mysterious.
They start to talk of factors beyond their control;
and they invent metaphors, like a 'fiscal black hole'.

They pretend they juggle figures, with great precision
and that everything they do is a 'difficult decision'.
But whatever they do, with this circumlocution
they return again and again, to the same solution:

A chancellor appears before us, preens and struts
then announces yet another set of public sector cuts.
We know what this means, even if they don't say –
fewer staff, worse conditions, and of course low pay.

It's not really a mystery, because it's always the same:
they wreck the economy and *we* get the blame.

THE ANNUAL EXAM GAME

Every year, we know it's always the same.
You and I know that for them it's a game.
Fiddling with examinations they say we need,
to ensure that education is up to speed.

They talk about something called 'comparability',
and that exams and tests measure ability.
Omitting to mention that they change the rules,
and that we won't notice because we're fools.

This year they thought they'd play a trump card:
they made key stage 2 reading much too hard.
'Oh that's not a problem, we'll find a way.
We'll change the pass mark,' they're bound to say.

So every year they pretend it's all objective,
when really we're in a system that's obstructive.
Hindering creative learning and investigation,
with exams and tests dominating education.

MATHS

I was sitting one morning, radio on, drinking tea
When I heard a voice, calling on me to agree
(well not just me, it was directed at the nation)
that it was time to shake up post-16 education.

That's funny, I thought, haven't there been bills and acts
which a secretary of state approves and enacts?
But here was Mr Sunak telling us what he'd thought up.
I nearly coughed up my tea back into my cup!

Maths! More Maths! The Prime minister demanded
I wondered if this is what he had commanded.
Is education now run to a brand new plan:
what gets taught is the whim of just one man?

What if post-16s would prefer other subjects?
And could it just be a person of that age objects?

And there's one other matter causing a laugh:
how's Rishi going to get all this new maths staff?

WHAT DO OUR MASTERS THINK OF US?

What do our masters think of us?
we sometimes wonder
And we would never know,
if it wasn't for a blunder.

We only get to know
how they write or speak,
if, there is, by chance,
some kind of a leak.

Have you heard of Matt Hancock,
the TV star?
He said, 'What a bunch of absolute arses
the teaching unions are.'

Gavin Williamson replied
(was it with a bit of a smirk?)
'I know they really really
do just hate work.'

They discussed whether teachers
would buy PPE
and Gavin and Matt
both seemed to agree:

'Some will just want to say
they can't...'
(How did they know?
Did they have a spy or plant?)

'...so they have an excuse to avoid
having to teach, what joys!!!'
(Did Gavin Williamson think,
teachers have time for such ploys?)

Gavin now says he was referring
to unions, not teachers,
so we think of them now
as kind, benign creatures.

ABSENCE MINDED

The trumpet was sounded, the rally was called,
the message went out to one and all:
not a day of school must ever be missed,
serial offenders must be put on a list.

A streaming cold can be no excuse.
If a parent asks, the school must refuse.
But then came the news, the word's on the street:
our schools are full of ropey concrete.

Pity the ministers with all their troubles
when they heard of concrete full of bubbles.
Well to tell the truth – now please don't groan –
as it turned out, they had always known.

So not a day must be lost when children are sick
Get 'em out of bed and into school quick.
But then they may find their classroom's a hut
Or they may even find that their school is shut.

School buildings: government to blame or not?
Or should we imagine that they just forgot?

DO WHAT YOU CAN

There's an amazing trick being prepared,
there will be no effort or money spared,
A plan will be carried out to the letter
and it's going to make education better.

You prick up your ears and wonder how.
You wonder if this plan's coming now?
But before you guess which way to bet
the details can't be revealed just yet.

All we can say on the government's behalf:
education will be provided with fewer staff
No matter the sincerity of the government's intention
We have a crisis in recruitment and retention.

But don't let that make you criticise the plan
Just get on with the job and do what you can.

WHO LOVES CHILDREN THE MOST?

Parents step forward and say,
'We love the child the most
we care for our children
more than we care for ourselves.'

Teachers step forward and say,
'We love the child the most
we educate children
so that they can play their part in the world.'

Doctors and nurses step forward and say
'We love the child the most
because we save their lives
and nurse them back to health.'

'Not so,' said a voice from the shadows.

Who's that? they wondered.
Who can love children more than
parents, teachers, doctors or nurses?

'It's me,' said the voice
and from out of the shadows,
stepped War.

TO MAKE EDUCATION BETTER

To make education better
it's often said
is why we're so lucky
to have Ofsted.

On no account say
that it's quite barmy
to have had a system
based on the army.

'Look out chaps!
Sergeant-major's here!'
Obedience forged
by the rule of fear.

Is it really
beyond imagination
to run education
through cooperation?

Experienced teachers
knowledgeable and wise
coming to schools
to discuss and advise.

But is there a rumour?
Perhaps an 'initiative'?
that education doesn't
have to be punitive.

Some people claiming to be educators
at their happiest when using calculators
reckon the way to develop this great nation
is to squeeze the arts out of education.

Of course they don't say such things directly,
they're schooled in how to do it correctly.
Did you notice how? Or perhaps you guessed:
they pulled the levers in how schools are assessed.

At a stroke of the pen, they changed the priorities
and once it reached the ear of the authorities,
student numbers doing arts courses dropped.
As a result, arts courses get chopped.

Please help us out, as we're simple fools:
is arts education now, just for private schools?

TIME FOR CHANGE?

So now's the time for many questions,
perhaps time too for many suggestions.
As they've said, it's the time for change
we're left wondering what they might arrange.

Some of us go back again and again
to the change that happened in 2010
when they heralded in a whole new plan
mostly (it seemed) because of just one man:

commands, orders, new laws and diktats
instructions, directives, parliamentary acts.
But if you have the power to run a nation
isn't there a better way to run education?

How about a start by talking to teachers?
After all, I've heard, they're not alien creatures.

SAME OLD STORY

A new government! So we expected a minimum:
they would set up a review of the old curriculum.

Good news came in. Indeed, they would.
They were listening. Would do what they could.

But how would they tap into teachers' thoughts?
Summon representatives? Read reports?

What about regional councils? Sharing ideas?
But proposals like these seem to provoke their fears.

So instead they did what they always do.
They set up a committee stuffed with you-know-who.

It's the same old story, top-down government
to get the advice that government want.

Other Books by Michael Rosen

In 1997 I completed a Ph.D. on the subject of authoring a piece of children's literature – a book of poems that was eventually published as *You Wait Till I'm Older Than You* (Puffin). In the thesis I tried to put to one side mystical and Romantic ideas around creating poetry and instead, locate the whole process in reality.

"This book brings together a big selection of Michael Rosen's writings and talks over five decades. They are about the centrality of literature, including children's literature, in the lives of all of us; about the power of poetry to inspire, console and entertain; and about the need to argue and campaign for these liberating forces in the face of ignorant and reductionist actions by successive governments in the United Kingdom."

John Richmond, Editor

This book is inspired by another book: *The Prince* by Niccolò Machiavelli in which Machiavelli appears to be giving a ruler advice on how to rule. Whether you take it at face value or as an ironic satire on cynical ways to maintain power is up to you. In 2023 and 2024, I thought I would have a go at doing something similar for what's going on now. Who or what these fables are about is for you to decide.

This booklet gathers together some recent talks and blogs on writing and reading, for use by teachers, librarians, parents, or anyone interested in engaging children and students in reading and writing, analysing why and how we do both.

POETRY AND STORIES
FOR PRIMARY AND LOWER
SECONDARY SCHOOLS

MICHAEL ROSEN

This is a short guide for teachers on how to teach poetry – reading, responding and writing. It is full of ideas on where and how to start, descriptions of why it's such a valuable activity. It's for you to use, adapt and change as you think best for the school and students you have in front of you.

WRITING
FOR
PLEASURE

MICHAEL ROSEN

This booklet is the third in a series about reading, writing and responding to literature. It focuses on how to make writing pleasurable and interesting and would be ideal as part of teacher training, staff discussion, curriculum development or just for reading and using.

READING FOR PLEASURE

MICHAEL ROSEN

This is a short guide for teachers on how to help a school put in place a reading for pleasure policy. To support this policy the guide also takes a close look at how children read – what do they think as they read? I've also included some plans from teachers putting reading for pleasure policies in place. It's for you to use, adapt and change as you think best for the school and students you have in front of you.

MICHAEL ROSEN'S POETRY VIDEOS: HOW TO GET CHILDREN WRITING AND PERFORMING POEMS TOO

JONNY WALKER
WITH
MICHAEL ROSEN

This is a guide for teachers on how to support children to write and perform poems that matter to them – it shares creative ways to harness the classroom potential of the 'Kids' Poems and Stories with Michael Rosen' YouTube channel. It is a practical and supportive handbook, put together by a practising teacher, and it suggests some ways that fellow teachers can create enriching writing communities with and for their students.

Further details on all these self-published books, including where they can be ordered from, can be found on my website:

www.michaelrosen.co.uk/books

www.ingramcontent.com/pod-product-compliance
Lightning Source LLC
Chambersburg PA
CBHW030458130626
46549CB00007B/2768